# PREFACE

When I minister, the Holy Spirit brings examples to help explain biblical truths. It may appear as if I am going down rabbit's trails but at the end it will bring clarity. I write the way I minister.

# ARE YOU A SHEEP OR A GOAT?

Will you hear Him say, "inherit the kingdom" or "depart from me, you cursed, into the eternal fire prepared for the devil and his angels"?

## The Fifth Letter of Apostle Andy From God to the Joshua Generation of 2022

### Written By
### Apostle Andrew Giannelli

Charleston, South Carolina

AG Production
Charleston, SC 29461
odm@homesc.com
Printed in the United States of America First Printing, 2022

# This Book Belongs To

**Date**

_______________

# Thank you for your support

**PRAYER:**

*And so, from the day we heard, we have not ceased to pray for you, asking that you may be filled with the knowledge of his will in all spiritual wisdom and understanding,* [10] *so as to walk in a manner worthy of the Lord, fully pleasing to him: bearing fruit in every good work and increasing in the knowledge of God;* [11]*being strengthened with all power, according to his glorious might, for all endurance and patience with joy;* [12] *giving thanks to the Father, who has qualified you to share in the inheritance of the saints in light.*

**Colossians 1:9-12 ESV**

**Apostle Andy to the Saints of the Joshua generation who are also faithful to God.**

**Apostle Andrew Giannelli**

## The Judgment of the Nations
## Matthew 25:31-46 RSV

*"When the Son of man comes in his glory, and all the angels with him, then he will sit on his glorious throne. 32 Before him will be gathered all the nations, and he will separate them one from another as a shepherd separates the sheep from the goats, 33 and he will place the sheep at his right hand, but the goats at the left.*

*34 Then the King will say to those at his right hand, 'Come, O blessed of my Father, inherit the kingdom prepared for you from the foundation of the world; 35 for I was hungry and you gave me food, I was thirsty and you gave me drink,*

I was a stranger and you welcomed me, *36* I was naked and you clothed me, I was sick and you visited me, I was in prison and you came to me.' *37* Then the righteous will answer him, 'Lord, when did we see thee hungry and feed thee, or thirsty and give thee drink? *38* And when did we see thee a stranger and welcome thee, or naked and clothe thee?

*39* And when did we see thee sick or in prison and visit thee?' *40* And the King will answer them, 'Truly, I say to you, as you did it to one of the least of these my brethren, you did it to me.' *41* Then he will say to those at his left hand, 'Depart from me, you cursed, into the eternal fire prepared for the devil and his angels; *42* for I was hungry and you gave me no food, I was thirsty and you gave me no drink, *43* I was a *stranger and you did not welcome me, naked and you did not clothe me, sick and in prison and you did not visit me.' 44 Then they also will answer, 'Lord, when did we see thee hungry or thirsty or a stranger or naked or sick or in prison, and did not minister to thee?' 45 Then he will answer them, 'Truly, I say to you, as you did it not to one of the least of these, you did it not to me.' 46 And they will go away into eternal punishment, but the righteous into eternal life."*

If that is what we are going to be judged on, why is it not being focused on and taught in most churches? I said most because some churches could be teaching on this, but I have not heard of one teaching on this in my 40 years of walking with God. This, however, was one of the first things God taught me when I was born again. God had me going to prison, helping poor people, and so on. I never put Matthew 7 before with Matthew 25.

## Matthew 7:19-24 WE

*Every tree that does not have good fruit is cut down and thrown into a fire. ²⁰ So you will know them by the things they do, good or bad fruit.' ²¹ Some people say to me, "Lord, Lord." But not all who say that will go into the king-dom of heaven. Only those who do what my Father in heaven wants, will go in. ²² Many peo-ple will say to me on that day, "Lord, Lord, did we not speak in your name? Did we not drive bad spirits out of people in your name? Did we not do big works in your name?" ²³ Then I will say to them, "I never knew you. Go away from me! What you do is very wrong!" 4 Everyone who hears what I say and obeys me will be like a man who has good sense. He built his house on a rock.*

## Matthew 7:19-24 AMP

*Every tree that does not bear good fruit is cut down and thrown into the fire. 20 Therefore, by their fruit you will recognize them [as false prophets]. 21 "Not everyone who says to Me, 'Lord, Lord,' will enter the kingdom of heaven, but only he who does the will of My Father who is in heaven. 22 Many will say to Me on that day [when I judge them], 'Lord, Lord, have we not prophesied in Your name, and driven out demons in Your name, and done many miracles in Your name?' 23 And then I will declare to them publicly, 'I never knew you; depart from Me* [you are banished from My presence], *you who act wickedly* [disregarding My commands].'

This also one of the first things I read, the book of Isaiah and found out that God was saying to do the same thing in the Old Testament.

## Isaiah 1:1-11 RSV

*The vision of Isaiah the son of Amoz, which he saw concerning Judah and Jerusalem in the days of Uzzi'ah, Jotham, Ahaz, and Hezeki'ah, kings of Judah.*

## The Wickedness of Judah

*Hear, O heavens, and give ear, O earth; for the Lord has spoken:" Sons have I reared and brought up, but they have rebelled against me ³The ox knows its owner, and the ass its master's* crib; but Israel does not know, my people does not understand. *4 Ah, sinful nation, a people laden with iniquity, offspring of evildoers, sons who deal corruptly! They have forsaken the Lord, they have despised the Holy One of Israel, they are utterly estranged. 5 Why will you still be smitten, that you continue to rebel? The whole head is sick, and the whole heart faint.*

*6 From the sole of the foot even to the head, there is no soundness in it, but bruises and sores and bleeding wounds; they are not pressed out, or bound up, or softened with oil. 7 Your country lies desolate, your cities are burned with fire; in your very presence aliens devour your land; it is desolate, as overthrown by aliens. 8 And the daughter of Zion is left like a booth in a vineyard, like a lodge in a cucumber field, like a besieged city. ⁹ If the Lord of hosts had not left us a few survivors, we should have been like Sodom, and become like Gomor'rah. ¹⁰ Hear the word of the Lord, you rulers of Sodom! Give ear to the teaching of our God, you people of Gomor'rah! ¹¹ "What to me is the multitude of your sacrifices? says the Lord;*

He is talking about what you have been told. You've been told to offer up a sacrifice of praise and told many more things to do to please God but have not been told to do what God wants as referred to in Matthew 25 or here in Isaiah as if praising God blesses God more than doing what Matthew 25 says to do for God. Whatever you do to the least you do to God, so if He is hungry just praise Him, but do not feed Him. Do you really think your praise means anything to Him when you do not feed Him or feed an orphan or widow or do the rest of what Matthew 25 says? You're being taught to praise Him with your mouth but not with your actions or works because the ministers are not instructing you and you're listening to them rather than God or reading the scriptures and allowing the Spirit of God teach you. Isaiah went on to say this for God. "Why aren't the prophets saying this today to the church and ministers?"

*"I have had enough of burnt offerings of rams and the fat of fed beasts; I do not delight in the blood of bulls, or of lambs, or of he-goats. ¹² "When you come to appear before me, who requires of you **this trampling of***

**<u>my courts?</u>** [13] *Bring no more vain offerings; incense is an abomination to me. New moon and* **<u>sabbath and the calling of assemblies</u>**— *I cannot endure iniquity and solemn assembly.*

## Isaiah 1:13 KJV

*Bring no more vain oblations; incense is an abomination unto me; the new moons and* **<u>sabbaths, the calling of assemblies,</u>** *I cannot away with; it is iniquity, even the solemn meeting.*

## Isaiah 1:12-13 TLB

*Who wants your sacrifices when you have no sorrow for your sins? The incense you bring me is a stench in my nostrils. Your holy celebrations of the new moon and* **<u>the Sabbath</u>**, *and* **<u>your special days for</u>**

**_fasting_**—*even **your** most pious meetings—* **_all are frauds_**! *I want nothing more to do with them.*

There is that word sabbath. It did not mean anything to God back then, and that was law back then. We are not under the law now. So, what does it really mean to God if you're going to church when He is not telling you to go to church, but instead you're listening to your flesh or a minister putting you under the law of the sabbath which means nothing to God?

The ministers and the denominations are manipulating you. Could be this Sunday, He wants you to feed a hungry person, or visit a widow, or orphan, and so on, maybe even help them financially or just spend a day with your family. Jesus never said tithe to a church, but

He did say Matthew 25. Maybe you should study all the scriptures on tithing yourself and ask God if He ever told a minister to have you tithe to a church? Many will say I do not know what I am talking about because they do not know themselves or want to keep manipulating you for your money. God can tell you to give to a church. It would not be a tithe but what God tells you to give.

I will say it again, tithe is a lie, and you know where liars are going. I will say it again, you have not been taught Matthew 25 from most pulpits. The word says **you** did these things in Matthew 25, not your church. Notice I said **your** church, not necessarily God's church. When it says seek ye first the kingdom of God, the word kingdom means the realm where God rules and reins.

If God is not ruling and reigning you, you are not in His kingdom. If you are not hearing and obeying God, you're not in His kingdom. If you're an ambassador for God, but you are not saying only what He says to say, doing only what He says to do, and going where God says to go, you are not representing Him. You're representing yourself or your organization.

## Isaiah 1:14 RSV

*Your new moons and your appointed feasts **my soul hates**; they have become **a burden to me**, I am weary of bearing them. [15] When you spread forth your hands, **I will hide my eyes from you**; even though you make many prayers, **I will not listen;** your hands are full of blood. [16] Wash yourselves; make yourselves clean; remove the evil of your doings from before* *my eyes; cease to do evil,* **¹⁷ learn to do good; seek justice, correct oppression; defend the fatherless, plead for the widow.** *¹⁸ "Come now, let us reason together, says the Lord: though your sins are like scarlet, they shall be as white as snow; though they are red like crimson, they shall become like wool.* **¹⁹ If you are willing and obedient, you shall eat the good of the land;**

This goes back to what God said when they came out of Egypt through

## Jeremiah 7:21-23 NASD

*This is what the Lord of armies, the God of Israel says: "Add your burnt offerings to your sacrifices and eat flesh. ²² For I did not speak to your fathers, or command them on the day that I brought them out of the land of Egypt, concerning burnt offerings and sacrific-es. 23 But this is the word what I commanded them, saying, 'Obey My voice, and I will be your God, and you will be My people; and you shall walk in all the word entirely in the way which I command you, so that it may go well for you.'*

## God Has Had Enough
## Isaiah 1:10-20 NASB

*Hear the word of the Lord, You rulers of Sodom; Listen to the instruction of our God, You people of Gomorrah! 11 "What are your many sacrifices to Me?" Says the Lord. "I have had enough of burnt offerings of rams And the fat of fattened cattle; And I take no pleasure in the blood of bulls, lambs, or goats. 12 When you come to appear before Me, Who requires of* you this trampling of My courtyards? ¹³ Do not go on bringing your worthless offerings, Incense is an abomination to Me. New moon and Sabbath, the proclamation of an assembly—I cannot endure wrongdoing and the festive assembly. ¹⁴ I hate your new moon festivals and your appointed feasts, They have become a burden to Me; I am tired of bearing them.

¹⁵ So when you spread out your hands in prayer, I will hide My eyes from you; Yes, even though you offer many prayers, I will not be listening. Your hands are covered with blood. ¹⁶ "Wash yourselves, make yourselves clean; Remove the evil of your deeds from My sight. Stop doing evil, ¹⁷ Learn to do good; Seek justice, Rebuke the oppressor, Obtain

*justice for the orphan, Plead for the widow's case.*

## Invitation to Debate

*"Come now, and let us debate your case, "Says the Lord, "Though your sins are as scarlet, They shall become as white as snow; Though they are red like crimson, They shall be like wool.* [19] ___If you are willing and obedient, You will eat the best of the land___*;* [20] *But if you refuse and rebel, You will be devoured by the sword. "For the mouth of the Lord has spoken.*

Isaiah was written in 732 BC. That's 2,753 years ago. That's 110 years before Jeremiah. What's sad is, God is having to say this again to the people of today because many prophets and other leaders are not saying what God wants them to say to God's people. If the ministers were saying what God was telling them to say, I would not have been told to write the letters God is telling me to write to this generation. God spoke to me and said most prophets are saying what God is going to do, but God wants to know what the prophets are going to do. They are not bringing correction, direction or building up the saints for the work of the ministry.

The prophet Isaiah said it in 732 BC. Jeremiah said it 622 BC. Why aren't the prophets today saying what Jeremiah and Isaiah said to warn the people to listen and obey God? That's all God wanted over 2,700 years ago, and that's all He wants today from His saints. Listen and obey. He said my sheep hear my voice and another they will not listen to. If you are not hearing His voice or being led by His Spirit, you can't obey God. What you are doing is being tossed to and fro, carried away by every wind of doctrine, by the cunning of men, by their craftiness in deceitful wiles. In other words, you are being manipulated by most of the leaders, denominations, and the devil. Why are they not speaking out against what is being taught about tithing, which is not of God, nor sabbath, or any other law you're being taught?

I want to repeat one more time over 2000 years ago, God said I required one thing, listen and obey. (Isaiah 1:19 and Jeremiah 7:23) Like I said before, God told me all the prophets are saying what God is going to do, but God wants to know what the prophets are going to do.

"Where there is no prophecy, my people cast off restraint." That means when my prophets don't tell the people what God is saying, the people cast off restraints. That includes all the ministers that don't say what God is telling them to say like Jesus said what the Father told Him to say. Jesus only told the people what God said to say, and He **was** the word. Remember, the Bible says the word killeth but the Spirit bringeth life.

If one does not bring correction, one does not walk in love which is the greatest out of faith, hope, and love.  If they don't say what God wants said, they don't fear God. They are walking in iniquity. In other words, violating the law, wickedness, or to sum it up disobeying what God says to an individual to do for God, doing it your way and not the way God says.  In other words, knowingly refusing to obey what God says to you, but instead doing your thing or what someone else is telling you to do.

## 1 Samuel 2:12-17 AMP
## The Sin of Eli's Sons

*The sons of Eli [Hophni and Phinehas] were[j] worthless (dishonorable, unprincipled) men; they did not know [nor respect] the Lord [13] and the custom of the priests with [the sacrifices of] the people. When any man was offering a sacrifice, the priest's servant would come while the meat was boiling, with a three-pronged [meat] fork in his hand; [14] then he would thrust it into the pan, or kettle, or caldron, or pot; everything that the fork brought up the priest would take for himself. This is what they did* in Shiloh to all [the sacrifices of] the Israelites who came there. ¹⁵ Also, before they burned (offered) the fat, the priest's servant would come and say to the man who was sacrificing, "Give the priest meat to roast, since he will not accept boiled meat from you, only raw."

¹⁶ If the man said to him, "Certainly they are to burn (offer) the fat first, and then you may take as much as you want," then the priest's servant would say, "No! You shall give it to me now or I will take it by force." ¹⁷ So the sin of the [two] young men [Hophni and Phinehas] was very great before the Lord, for the men treated the offering of the Lord disrespectfully.

In the book of Malachi in the bible, Malachi was talking about the priest robbing God, not the people. The Tithe was only given from crops grown and livestock. Never was any person told to tithe earned income. Why are the prophets today not speaking against the lie of the tithe? The law of the sabbath? If God told Ezekiel "If they die in their sin, I will demand your blood for theirs.

If you do not warn them. It will be against you.", will God not say this for all the prophets who are not coming against the false teaching of the tithe and the lack of teaching on being led by the Spirit and being taught by the Comforter?

## 1 Samuel 2:22-36 AMP
## Eli Rebukes His Sons

*Now Eli was very old; and he heard about everything that his sons were doing to all [the people of] Israel, and how they were lying with the women who served at the entrance to the Tent of Meeting (tabernacle).* ²³ *Eli said to them, "Why do you do such things, the evil things that I hear from all these people?* ²⁴ *No, my sons; for the report that I keep hearing from the passers-by among the Lord's people is not good.* ²⁵ *If one man does wrong and sins against another, God will intercede (arbitrate) for him; but if a man does wrong to the Lord, who can intercede for him?"* **_But they would not listen to their father, for it was the Lord's will to put them to death._**

²⁷ *Then a man of God (prophet) came to Eli and said to him, "Thus says the Lord: 'Did I not plainly reveal Myself to the house of your father (ancestor) when they were in Egypt in bondage to Pharaoh's house?* ²⁸ *Moreover, I*

selected him out of all the tribes of Israel to be My priest, to go up to My altar, to burn incense, to wear an ephod before Me. And [from then on] I gave to the house of your father all the fire offerings of the sons of Israel. 29 Why then do you kick at (despise) My sacrifice and My offering which I commanded in My dwelling place, and honor your sons more than Me, by fattening yourselves with the choicest part of every offering of My people Israel?'

30 Therefore the Lord God of Israel declares, 'I did indeed say that your house and that of [Aaron] your father would walk [in priestly service] before Me forever.' But now the Lord declares, 'Far be it from Me—**for those who honor Me I will honor, and those who despise Me will be insignifi-**

**cant and contemptible.** *³¹ Behold, the time is coming when I will cut off your strength and the strength of your father's house, so that there will not be an old man in your house.*

*³² You will look at the distress of My house (the tabernacle), in spite of all the good which God will do for Israel, and there will never again be an old man in your house. ³³ Yet I will not cut off every man of yours from My altar; your eyes will fail from weeping and your soul will grieve, and all those born in your house will die as men [in the prime of life].*

*³⁴ This will be the sign to you which shall come concerning your two sons, Hophni and Phinehas: on the same day both of them shall die. ³⁵ But I will raise up for Myself a faithful priest who will do according to what is in*

*My heart and in My soul; and I will build him a permanent and enduring house, and he will walk before My anointed] forever.* ³⁶ *And it will happen that everyone who is left in your house will come and bow down to him for a piece of silver and a loaf of bread and say, "Please assign me to one of the priest's offices so I may eat a piece of bread."*

## 1 Samuel 3:10-14 AMP

*Then the Lord came and stood and called as at the previous times, "Samuel! Samuel!" Then Samuel answered, "Speak, for Your servant is listening." ¹¹ The Lord said to Samuel, "Behold, I am about to do a thing in Israel at which both ears of everyone who hears it will ring. ¹² On that day I will carry out against Eli everything that I have spoken concerning his house (family), from beginning to end. ¹³ Now I have told him that I am about to judge his house forever for the sinful behavior which he knew [was happening], because his sons were bringing a curse on themselves [dishonoring and blaspheming God] and he did not rebuke them. ¹⁴ Therefore I have sworn to the house of Eli that the sinful behavior of Eli's house (family) shall not be atoned for by sacrifice or offering forever."*

The leaders and prophets have been spoken to by God, but they have not brought correction. God is raising up some Samuels in the Joshua generation to bring correction. It appears to me that Eli did not fear God and would not bring correction even though He knew what was happening in his house. Many leaders and

Prophets know what is going on, but God told me this morning, they do not fear God. They are not bringing correction to the body of believers and are not correcting or judging the prophetic word coming forth.

Let's look at **Ezekiel 3:16-21 TLB**

*At the end of the seven days, the Lord said to me: 17 "Son of dust, I have appointed you as a watchman for Israel; whenever I send my people a warning, pass it on to them at once. 18 If you refuse to warn the wicked when I want you to tell them, 'You are under the penalty of death; therefore, repent and save your life,' they will die in their sins, but I will punish you. I will demand your blood for theirs. 19 But if you warn them, and they keep on sinning and refuse to repent, they will die in their sins, but you are blameless—you have done all you could. ²⁰ And if a good man becomes bad, and you refuse to warn him of the consequences, and the Lord destroys him, his previous good deeds won't help him— he shall die in his sin.* **<u>But I will hold you responsible for his death and punish you</u>**. *²¹ But if you warn him and he repents, he shall live, and you have saved your own life too."*

If you read Ezekiel, you will see he was continually telling the people what God told him to say. All the prophets I hear today are saying what God is going to do, but what are they doing and saying? That is what God wants to know. Please learn to fear God. Do not be like those in the Bible and present-day ministers who do not fear God.

## Jeremiah 7 :21-26 RSV

*Thus says the Lord of hosts, the God of Israel: "Add your burnt offerings to your sacrifices and eat the flesh. ²² For in the day that I brought them out of the land of Egypt, I did not speak to your fathers or command them concerning burnt offerings and sacrifices.*

*²³ But this command I gave them, '***Obey my voice, and I will be your God, and you shall be my people; and walk in all the way that I command you, that it may be well with you.***' ²⁴ But they did not obey or incline their ear, but walked in their own counsels and the stubbornness of their evil hearts, and went backward and not forward. ²⁵ From the day that your fathers came out of the land of Egypt to this day, I have persistently sent* *all my servants the prophets to them, day after day; [26] yet they did not listen to me, or incline their ear, but stiffened their neck. They did worse than their fathers.*

**Jeremiah** did not say do what the leaders have been telling you today to do and I will be your God. Adam was separated from God because of disobedience. What makes you think you can just do whatever you want or what someone tells you and still God will be your God? Man is telling you that, not God. Read Matthew 25 again.

Jeremiah was written 2,644 years ago, 622 years before Christ. That is how long God has been saying this, but you are not being told to OBEY HIS VOICE. Your offerings and sacrifices including your money does nothing for Him. He wants you to hear what He says and obey. He did not say obey His word, but He said obey His voice. You cannot please Him any other way. Your goal should be to listen to God and obey. We have this story in the Old Testament so we will not do the same things they did thinking they were pleasing God.

Do you realize how much more accountable you will be if you are listening to man and not God's voice and doing what man or flesh is telling you instead of doing what God is telling you to do?

God created Adam and put in Adam all he needed to fulfill God's purpose for him. He has done the same in you. He has put in you all you need to fulfill God's divine will for you; to accomplish His purpose, not someone else's purpose for you. Quit listening to leaders and listen to God. Because of Jesus's death, burial, and resurrection, we can walk and talk with God like Adam did before sinning. When we accept Jesus we have the right to walk and talk with God like Adam did. Jesus undid what Adam did. We have been reconciled to God by Jesus.

The veil to the Holy of Holies was ripped from top to bottom so that you can go before God for yourself. You do not need a priest or a minister to go before God for you. We can walk as sons of God. All we have to do is be led by the Spirit, not a man.

If you are not being taught that, get out of where you are and follow your Heavenly Shepherd now before it is too late. He will homeschool you. Most schools and churches are keeping you from truly knowing and fully following God.

I can see Jesus sitting next to the Father in Heaven and saying, "Father I do not understand. They know You sent me to die for them, and they confess that. They say they have faith in me. They praise Me and say all kinds of good things about Me, but when I am hungry, they do not give Me food, when I am thirsty, they do not give Me a drink, when I am a stranger, they do not welcome Me, when I am naked they do not clothe Me, when I am sick, they do not visit Me, when I am in prison they do not come to Me, and they do not visit the widows and orphans, which is pure religion. That means religion can't get any better than that. That's our priority for the saints, but the minister's priority for them is not the same as ours. We left them a Bible so they can do what it says to do. You said I needed to come to Heaven so You could send the comforter to teach them, and they would have need that no man teaches them.

We also left them the Apostles, Prophets, Evangelist, Pastors, and Teachers to build them up, but they are not doing that for the saints but instead focusing on their vision instead of their purpose from Us for the upbuilding of the body that We assigned them. The saints are not doing these things but doing what the ministers and priest are telling them to do or doing what they want to do. I just do not understand how they can say they love Me but will not listen to Us, the word, or the Spirit.

The Bible says in **1 John 2:26-27 TLB**

*These remarks of mine about the Antichrist are pointed at those who would dearly love to blindfold you and lead you astray. [27] But you have received the Holy Spirit, and he lives within you, in your hearts, so that you don't need anyone to teach you what is right. For he teaches you all things, and he is the Truth, and no liar; and so, just as he has said, you must live in Christ, never to depart from him.*

*They even hear My voice but will not follow Me. My sheep hear my voice, why won't they follow Me? I also told them all that the Father has is mine and I will reveal it to you by the Spirit, but it seems to me, they count on the ministers and their denominations more than the Spirit. It really seems to me, Father, that*

the ministers are keeping people from knowing and being led by the Holy Spirit because
they have the people counting on them rather
than the Holy Spirit. I must assume, the ministers don't know how to count on the Holy
Spirit. Otherwise, they wouldn't get between
the people and the Holy Spirit."

## Jeremiah 7:21-23 TLB

*The Lord, the God of Israel says: Away with
your offerings and sacrifices! [22] It wasn't offerings and sacrifices I wanted from your fathers
when I led them out of Egypt. That was not the
point of my command. [23] But what I told them
was: <u>Obey me, and I will be your God and you
shall be my people; only do as I say, and all
shall be well!</u>*

I want to repeat, that was over 2644 years ago, and God is still saying the same thing, "one thing I require, listen and obey." However, the ministers are teaching people all kinds of things and avoiding teaching the people to listen and obey the voice of the Lord.  Can you understand? This is all He wants. Just listen and obey. Even in church services, shut up, quit doing what you want to do, and listen and obey.

If every church service is the same every time you go to church, it is not pleasing to God. It might be pleasing to you and your ministers, but they are not letting God lead the service, their flesh is. It's just like in the Bible, when Jesus wanted to do something in the synagogues, they let Him do a little. He could have done so much more, but they wouldn't let Him.

In many church services today, they will not let God do what He wants to do in the services.

Over twenty-five years ago, God told me to stop laying hands on people, and then He told me, "I told Moses to speak to the rock, but he hit it. He would not glorify Me by doing it My way. It caused him and all the people in the wilderness to not go into what I had promised them." Then God told me, everywhere I send my apostles, I confirmed the word with signs and wonders. Not one time in over twenty-five years has God not confirmed what He told me to say in church services and anywhere else He has me go to pray for people.

In one service in the Dominican Republic, when they asked me to come up and minister. As I was walking up to the pulpit God said,

"Do not say a word until I tell you to speak. If they close the service and I have not told you to speak, do not even speak in the car when you leave here." Thirty minutes went by. The pastor and my interpreter brought a man to me who had a stroke outside. They wanted me to pray for him. I shook my head no, so they laid him on the altar. Ten minutes later, God said "You can speak now." I asked the people, "Is this God's house?" They said, "Yes." I asked, "Could anyone tell me since you have been in God's house today, have you done anything God told you to do or say?" Everyone got quiet. I taught when we come into God's house, we need to do what He says or shows us to do, not what we want to do or what our plan or program is. Then I went on and ministered. The man lying on the altar who had the stroke came to my interpreter and wanted to say something. So, I let him. He said, "When they laid me on the altar, I knew I was going to die. But when this man started talking, Jesus stood in front of me. He walked up to me, touched me, then healed me." This is what God told me, "If I would obey Him, by saying and doing what He tells me or shows me, He would confirm His word with signs and wonders." Who got the glory when the man testified? That is correct, God.

Too many ministers with signs and wonders like Moses are not glorifying God but taking His glory for themselves and not equipping the saints to do what God has anointed them to do. So, the ministers get all the recognition for what God is doing through them, not by them. It is like a hose taking credit for the water flowing through it. The hose is just the conduit the water is traveling through. The way you have always done things can keep you back from following what God wants you to come into or advance to and can send you to hell.

I was confident I heard from God. I felt like the Apostles when they had a few fish and loaves of bread. God told them to split amongst them what was in their hands, walk toward people sitting in groups of fifty, and feed them from their two little hands full of food. I did what He told me to do and just like the food multiplied to feed the five thousand, God did what He told me He was going to do. He confirmed His word with a sign and wonder. I have been doing what He said for over twenty-five years.

I just thought of this, how many pastors would put someone in the pulpit and let forty minutes go by and not do something about the minister not saying anything for 40 minutes?

## Jeremiah 7:24-34 TLB

*24 But they wouldn't listen; they kept on doing whatever they wanted to, following their own stubborn, evil thoughts. They went backward instead of forward.*

*25 Ever since the day your fathers left Egypt until now, I have kept on sending them my prophets, day after day.*

I believe when God said to me, the prophets are all saying what I'm going to do but I want to know what they are going to do, God was referring to why aren't the prophets telling the people what I'm telling them to say to the people from Me instead of just talking about what I'm going to do.

*²⁶ But they wouldn't listen to them or even try to hear.*

This is what most ministers are doing to God right now. They will not listen to the Holy Spirit or even try to listen or teach the people to listen to the Holy Spirit, so God gets glorified. They keep saying the word says, the word says, the word says. Let me point our here that Jesus was the word, and He only said what the Father told Him to say and did what He saw the Father doing.

Who are these ministers today that can just quote scriptures to prove what they want to prove, teach what they want to teach, do what they want to do, but not allow the Holy Spirit to lead and guide or let God do what He wants to do in a service? I want to repeat again, God gave the ministers as a gift or present to the saints to build them up. If they are not doing that, building up the saints for what God has called the saints to do, thus sayeth the Lord, "Those ministers not building up the saints are going to hell." They are hard and stubborn and rebellious—worse even than their fathers were.

*27 Tell them everything that I will do to them, but don't expect them to listen. Cry out your warnings, but don't expect them to respond.*

God is telling me that all the Moses ministers of today are going to have the same response as in verse 27 when they read this letter.

*28 Say to them: "This is the nation that*

*refuses to obey the Lord its God and refuses to be taught. She continues to live a lie."*

God is also saying verse 28 about the Moses ministers. Nations here in this verse, refers to today's Moses ministers. They refuse to be led by the Holy Spirit and allow God to do what He wants in the churches so God gets the glory not the ministers or denominations, etc.

*29 O Jerusalem, shave your head in shame and weep alone upon the mountains; for the Lord has rejected and forsaken this people of his wrath. 30 For the people of Judah have sinned before my very eyes, says the Lord. They have set up their idols right in my own Temple, polluting it. 31 They have built the altar called Topheth in the valley of Ben-hinnom,* and there they burn to death their little sons and daughters as sacrifices to their gods—a deed so horrible I've never even thought of it, let alone commanded it to be done. ³² The time is coming, says the Lord, when that valley's name will be changed from Topheth or Ben-hinnom Valley, to the Valley of Slaughter; for there will be so many slain to bury that there won't be room enough for all the graves, and they will dump the bodies in that valley.

³³ The bodies of my people shall be food for the birds and animals, and no one shall be left to scare them away. ³⁴ I will end the happy singing and laughter and the joyous voices of the bridegrooms and brides in the streets of Jerusalem and in the cities of Judah. For the land shall lie in desolation.

## **2 Corinthians 5:17-21 ESV**

*Therefore, if anyone is in Christ, he is a new creation. The old has passed away; behold, the new has come. [18] All this is from God, who through Christ reconciled us to himself and gave us the ministry of reconciliation;*

*[19] that is, in Christ God was reconciling the world to himself, not counting their trespasses against them, and entrusting to us the message of reconciliation.*

*[20] Therefore, we are ambassadors for Christ, God making his appeal through us. We implore you on behalf of Christ, be reconciled to God. [21] For our sake he made him to be sin who knew no sin, so that in him we might become the righteousness of God.*

## Isaiah 1:20-31 AMP

*But if you refuse and rebel, You shall be devoured by the sword." For the mouth of the Lord has spoken.* **Zion Corrupted, to Be Redeemed**

*21 How the faithful city has become a prostitute [idolatrous, despicable], She who was full of justice! Right standing with God once lodged in her, But now murderers. 22 Your silver has turned to lead, Your wine is diluted with water.*

*23 Your rulers are rebels and companions of thieves; Everyone loves bribes and chases after gifts.* ***They do not defend the fatherless, Nor does the widow's cause come before them [instead they delay or turn a deaf ear.***

Here it is again. They wouldn't take care of the fatherless and the widows. God has been saying this a long time, and you will be judged for this one day. Your excuse will not be, "the ministers never told me." You make your minister your shepherd, but like David, you should know the Lord as your shepherd, not a man. Even though many of the ministers tell you they are your shepherd, it's not true. They're supposed to be leading you to God's pasture, not theirs.

I'll say it again, the Bible says you have need that no man teacheth you, but the Holy Spirit will teach you. More than likely, you have not been taught that. The curtain was rent to the Holy of Holies from the top to the bottom by God so you can approach God yourself. You don't need a priest or any other kind of minister to approach God for you. You can go into God's presence yourself. Jesus died for you to reconcile you to God so you can go to God yourself. What if you had children and they would not come talk to you because someone was telling them they had to go to them to receive from you. How would you feel toward that person or group of people? That is how God is feeling toward all the leaders keeping His children, that Jesus died for, from going to God.

*24 Therefore the Lord God of hosts, The Mighty One of Israel, declares: "Ah, I will be freed of My adversaries and avenge Myself on My enemies. 25 "And I will turn My hand against you And will [thoroughly] purge away your dross as with lye* and remove all your tin (impurity). ²⁶ "Then I will restore your judges as at the first, and your counselors as at the beginning; Afterward you will be called the city of righteousness, The faithful city." ²⁷ Zion will be redeemed with justice and her repentant ones with righteousness. ²⁸ But rebels and sinners will be crushed and destroyed together, and those who abandon (turn away from) the Lord will be consumed (perish). ²⁹ For you will be ashamed [of the degradation] of the oaks in which you took [idolatrous] pleasure, And you will be ashamed of the gardens [of passion] which you have chosen [for pagan worship]. ³⁰ For you will be like an oak whose leaf withers and dies and like a garden that has no water. ³¹ The strong man will become *tinder, and his work a spark. So both will burn together and there will be none to quench them.*

## False and True Worship
## Isaiah 58:1-13 (RSV)

*"Cry aloud, spare not, lift up your voice like a trumpet; declare to my people their transgression, to the house of Jacob their sins. ² Yet they seek me daily, and delight to know my ways, as if they were a nation that did righteousness and did not forsake the ordinance of their God; they ask of me righteous judgments, they delight to draw near to God. ³ 'Why have we fasted, and thou seest it not? Why have we humbled ourselves, and thou takest no knowledge of it?' Behold, in the day of your fast you seek your own pleasure, Or pursue your*

own business and oppress all your workers. 4 Behold, you fast only to quarrel and to fight and to hit with wicked fist. Fasting like yours this day will not make your voice to be heard on high. 5 Is such the fast that I choose, a day for a man to humble himself? Is it to bow down his head like a rush, and to spread sackcloth and ashes under him? Will you call this a fast, and a day acceptable to the Lord? 6 **"Is not this the fast that I choose: to loose the bonds of wickedness to undo the thongs of the yoke, to let the oppressed go free, and to break every yoke? 7 Is it not to share your bread with the hungry, and bring the homeless poor into your house; when you see the naked, to cover** *him, and not to hide yourself from your own flesh?*

*This means to me when you look in the mirror see what you are and go to God and confess your flesh is not doing what it should be doing and ask God for help.*

Most ministers today say, "Your blessing is coming when you support what we are doing.", but God does not say that. When have you heard a minister say what God says in verse 6 and 7? Now, read the blessings of **doing** verse 6 and 7.

[8] <u>*Then shall your light break forth like the dawn, and your healing shall spring up speedily; your righteousness shall go before you, the glory of*</u>

**_the Lord shall be your rear guard._ _<sup>9</sup> Then you shall call, and the Lord will answer; you shall cry, and he will say, Here I am._**

"If you take away from the midst of you the yoke, the pointing of the finger, and speaking wickedness, **<sup>10</sup> if you pour yourself out for the hungry and satisfy the desire of the afflicted,** then shall your light rise in the darkness and your gloom be as the noonday.<sup>11</sup> And the Lord will guide you continually, and satisfy your desire with good things, and make your bones strong; and you shall be like a watered garden, like a spring of water, whose waters fail not. <sup>12</sup> And your ancient ruins shall be rebuilt; you shall raise up the foundations of many generations; you shall be called the *repairer of the breach, the restorer of streets to dwell in.* ¹³ *"If you turn back your foot from the sabbath, from doing* **<u>your pleasure</u>** *Or business on my holy day, and call the sabbath a delight and the holy day of the Lord honorable; if you honor it, not going your own ways, or seeking your own pleasure, Or* **pursuing your own business** *or talking idly;*

What did Jesus, our example, do on the sabbath? That's right, the Father's business. He said my Father and I still worketh. You see most are going to church because that is what they have been taught, to keep the sabbath day. It means do what God tells you to do by the Spirit. If you are born again, every day should be a sabbath to you to do God's will not yours. Most go to church for the fellowship, praising, prayer, and so on. This is what **they** want, not what the Father wants. It is in sowing we reap. He wants obedience to the Holy Spirit which is the highest form of praise.

If when you ask God on your sabbath, "What should I do today?", and He tells you, then do what He tells you. Be led by the Spirit not anything else. Hear God and Obey. You cannot obey God if you are not talking and listening to Him. He said my house shall be a house of prayer for all people. God told me, that meant everyone He sends in His building the same way Burger King cooks hamburgers for everyone who comes in the door.

## Isaiah 29:13-14 RSV

*And the Lord said: "Because this people draw near with their mouth and honor me with their lips, while their hearts are far from me, and their fear of me is a commandment of men learned by rote; ¹⁴ therefore, behold, I will again do marvelous things with this people, wonderful and marvelous; and the wisdom of their wise men shall perish, and the discernment of their discerning men shall be hid.*

## ESV Isaiah 58:14 ESV

*Then you shall take delight in the Lord, and I will make you ride upon the heights of the earth; I will feed you with the heritage of Jacob your father, for the mouth of the Lord has spoken."*

Are you a sheep or Goat? If God said back in Jeremiah, "Obey My voice.", how much more today, with the Holy Spirit as our teacher, do you believe God requires us to obey His voice?

Most are not being taught this.

God never ordained a denomination. Yet many are doing and believing what their denomination says to do and believe but are not being led by the Spirit or following God's voice. They are being eclipsed from God by man. God is saying, "I have had enough of what has been going on." Like in Sodom, He has heard the cries of the people and is coming down.

## John 10:26-30 AMP

*But you do not believe Me [so you do not trust and follow Me] because you are not My sheep. [27] The sheep that are My own hear My voice and listen to Me; I know them, and they follow Me. [28] And I give them eternal life, and they will never, ever [by any means] perish; and no one will ever snatch them out of My* hand. ²⁹ *My Father, who has given them to Me, is greater and mightier than all; and no one is able to snatch them out of the Father's hand. ³⁰ I and the Father are One [in essence and nature]."*

Are you hearing His voice? Are you being taught to hear His voice and be led by the Spirit? **If not, you are being led astray by the minister or denomination you are under.**

### John 3:36 RSV

*He who believes in the Son has eternal life;* ***he who does not obey the Son shall not see life, but the wrath of God rests upon him.***

When it says believe it includes obedience to the Son. If you do not obey, you do not believe.

Let me say here many ministers think they are something because of signs and wonders.

## Matthew 13:58 RSV

*And he did not many mighty works there because of their unbelief.*

This word unbelief means *unfaithfulness, to be rebelliously disobedient.* Note it says He did not do, it does not say He could not do. Many ministers say because they did not have faith, Jesus could not do many mighty works. That is not what it says in any version of the Bible that I look up. So many say, "If you just had faith God would heal you, you lack faith." To that, I ask people how much faith did Lazarus have? They usually say, "Well, that was Jesus." So, I ask them, "Well, how much faith did the bones have in Ezekiel 37?" Here is where God wants you to see that Ezekiel just said what God said to say, and it happened. Too many are using their gifts for manifestation for people instead of being directed by God. The ministers have forgotten they are **<u>a gift from Jesus to the saints to build the saints up for the work that God has anointed the saints to do,</u>** not to build up their reputation and following. Jesus could have done more signs and wonders but did not because the Father did not direct Him to. You must realize Jesus could have come off the cross, but His cup was to die for you and me. You see, most ministers today will not get on the cross God has for them and die for others to build others up for what God has anointed them to do for God. They want to keep getting recognition from man. They like the praises of man rather the praises of God. The same way God used Ezekiel He wants to use you. He wants you to hear His voice and only say what God tells you to say.

## John 12:43 RSV

*for they loved the praise of men more than the praise of God.*

Note here, that God must have praised them at times for them to say this. Has God ever praised you? God would rather praise you then you praise Him. What do you welcome more, your children praising you, or you being able to praise them for their obedience?

## John 10:41 AMP

*Many came to Him, and they were saying, "John did not perform a single sign (attesting miracle), but everything John said about this Man was true and accurate."*

## Luke 7:25-28 ESV

*But what did you go out to see? A man dressed in soft clothing [entirely unsuited for the harsh wilderness]? Those who wear splendid clothing and live in luxury are in royal palaces! 26 But what did you [really] go out to see? A prophet? Yes, I say to you, and one far more [eminent and remarkable] than a prophet [who foretells the future].*

*27 This is the one of whom it is written [by the prophet Malachi], 'Behold, I send My messenger ahead of You, Who will prepare Your way before You.' 28 I tell you, among those born of women there is no one greater than John; yet he who is least in the kingdom of God is greater [in privilege] than he."*

The kingdom, as I said before, is where God rules and reigns in your life. Read my book on Elijah, and you will see how many are using their anointing instead of being obedient to what God says to do. The scriptures say John did no signs, but Jesus said,

## Luke 7:28 ESV

*I tell you, among those born of women there is no one greater than John; yet the one who is least in the kingdom of God is greater than he.*

None was greater than John. Many people have bragged on men and women in the Old Testament, but Jesus bragged on John. Think about that a few minutes and try to understand why Jesus bragged on John. Then try to do better than John did.

## Revelation 19:7-8 RSV

*Let us rejoice and exult and give him the glory, for the marriage of the Lamb has come, and his Bride has made herself ready; ⁸ it was granted her to be clothed with fine linen, bright and pure"—for the fine linen is the righteous deeds of the saints.*

The King James Version says righteousness of the saints. Study the word and find that it means righteous deeds. The Bible is not talking about grace, but righteous deeds. Matthew 25 confirms it is deeds of the sheep, *"and the King will say Come oh blessed of My Father, inherit the kingdom prepared for you from the foundation of the world."* **Matthew 25:34**

For those who think the KJV is the only one, here are some samples. If you look up righteousness in the Strong's concordance, you will see in this verse it is righteous deeds.

## Revelation 19:8 NIV

*"Fine linen, bright and clean, was given her to wear.' (Fine linen stands for the righteous acts of God's holy people.)"*

## Revelation 19:8 ESV

*"it was granted her to clothe herself with fine linen, bright and pure"—for the fine linen is the righteous deeds of the saints."*

## Revelation 19:8 KJV

*"And to her was granted that she should be arrayed in fine linen, clean and white: for the fine linen is the righteousness of saints."*

## Revelation 19:8 NASB

*"It was given to her to clothe herself in fine*

*linen, bright and clean; for the fine linen is the righteous acts of the saints."*

## Revelation 19:8 NLT

*"She has been given the finest of pure white linen to wear.' For the fine linen represents the good deeds of God's holy people."*

## Revelation 19:8 CSB

*"She was given fine linen to wear, bright and pure. For the fine linen represents the righteous acts of the saints."*

Read Matthew 25 again. These are righteous deeds, and so is **James 1:27 RSV**.

*Religion that is pure and undefiled before God and the Father is this: to visit orphans and widows in their affliction, and to keep oneself unstained from the world.*

Remember it talks about this in Isaiah chapter 1. Have you been taught this by your minister?

What did Job say 3,988 years ago?

### ESV Job 31:16-23 ESV

*"If I have withheld anything that the poor desired, or have caused the eyes of the widow to fail, [17] or have eaten my morsel alone, and the fatherless has not eaten of it [18] (for from my youth the fatherless grew up with me as with a father, and from my mother's womb I guided the widow), [19] if I have seen anyone perish for lack of clothing, or the needy without covering, [20] if his body has not blessed me, and if he was not warmed with the fleece of my sheep [21] if I have raised my hand against the fatherless, because I saw my help in the gate, [22] then*

*let my shoulder blade fall from my shoulder, and let my arm be broken from its socket* ²³ *For I was in terror of calamity from God, and I could not have faced his majesty.*

Why would he say this if God had not instilled in them 3,988 years ago to do these things? If God expected that of them 3,988 years ago, why would He not expect this of you today? I will say it again, have you been taught this as a –God expected work from you personally- by your ministers?

## Ezekiel 18:7,9 ESV

⁷*does not oppress anyone, but restores to the debtor his pledge, commits no robbery,* **_gives his bread to the hungry and covers the naked with a garment,_**

⁹ *walks in my statutes and is careful to*

*observe my ordinances—__he is righteous,__ he shall surely live, says the Lord God.*

## Ezekiel 18:16 RSV

*does not wrong anyone, exacts no pledge, commits no robbery, but gives his bread to the hungry and covers the naked with a garment,*

You see that word righteous? That's where the righteous deeds in Revelation comes from. You get to wear fine linen, bright and pure for the fine linen is the righteous deeds of the saints. God expected this 2,614 years ago, how much more today seeing as we are under a better covenant? I will say it again, have you been taught this as a God expected work from you personally? Most are saying today it is just grace. Grace without works is dead the bible says. Do you mean "faith" here?

## Hebrew 13:1-3 RSV

*Let brotherly love continue. ² Do not neglect to show hospitality to strangers, for thereby some have entertained angels unawares. ³ Remember those who are in prison, as though in prison with them; and those who are ill-treated, since you also are in the body.*

## Luke 3:7-11 RSV

*He said therefore to the multitudes that came out to be baptized by him, "You brood of vipers! Who warned you to flee from the wrath to come? ⁸ <u>Bear fruits that befit repentance,</u> and do not begin to say to yourselves, 'We have Abraham as our father'; for I tell you, God is able from these stones to raise up children to Abraham. ⁹ Even now the axe is laid to the root of the trees; every tree therefore that does* not bear good fruit is cut down and thrown into the fire." [10] And the multitudes asked him, "What then shall we do?" [11] And he answered them, "He who has two coats, let him share with him who has none; and he who has food, let him do likewise."

## Faith without Works Is Dead
## James 2:14-26 ESV

What good is it, my brothers, if someone says he has faith but does not have works? Can that faith save him? [15] If a brother or sister is poorly clothed and lacking in daily food, [16] and one of you says to them, "Go in peace, be warmed and filled," without giving them the things needed for the body, what good is that? [17] So also faith by itself, if it does not have works, is dead.

¹⁸ *But someone will say, "You have faith and I have works." Show me your faith apart from your works, and I will show you my faith by my works.* ¹⁹ *You believe that God is one; you do well. Even the demons believe—and shudder!* ²⁰ *Do you want to be shown, you foolish person, that faith apart from works is useless?* ²¹ <u>Was not Abraham our father justified by works when he offered up his son Isaac on the altar?</u>*

²² *You see that faith was active along with his works, and faith was completed by his works;* ²³ *and the Scripture was fulfilled that says, "Abraham believed God, and it was counted to him as righteousness"—and he was called a friend of God.* ²⁴ *You see that a person is justified by works and not by faith alone.* ²⁵ *And in*

*the same way was not **<u>also Rahab the prostitute justified by works</u>** when she received the messengers and sent them out by another way? <sup>26</sup> For as the body apart from the spirit is dead, so also faith apart from works is dead.*

I believe Lot was regarded as righteous for taking in the two angels which were sojourners just as Rahab was for hiding the two spies. Look at the favor she and her family got because of her good deed.

## James 1:26-27 ESV

*If anyone thinks he is religious and does not bridle his tongue but deceives his heart, this person's religion is worthless. <sup>27</sup> **Religion that is pure and undefiled before God the Father is this: to visit orphans and*** *widows in their affliction, and to keep oneself unstained from the world.*

**When was the last time you heard this preached? Line this up with Mathew 25. When was the last time you visited an orphan or widow? Compare that with the many times you have been told you need to be in church and give money but have not been told anything about giving to widows and orphans. It does not say going to church, tithing, praising, winning souls or anything else you are being taught is pure religion, does it?**

**James 1:19-25 ESV**
**Hearing and Doing the Word**

*Know this, my beloved brothers: let every person be quick to hear, slow to speak, slow to* anger; [20] *for the anger of man does not produce the righteousness of God.* [21] *Therefore put away all filthiness and rampant wickedness and receive with meekness the implanted word, which is able to save your souls.* [22] *But be doers of the word, and not hearers only, deceiving yourselves.* [23] *For if anyone is a hearer of the word and not a doer, he is like a man who looks intently at his natural face in a mirror.*

[24] *For he looks at himself and goes away and at once forgets what he was like.* [25] *But the one who looks into the perfect law, the law of liberty, and perseveres, being no hearer who forgets but a doer who acts, he will be blessed in his doing.*

## 2 Timothy 1:16-18 RSV

*May the Lord grant mercy to the household*

*of Onesiph'orus, for he often refreshed me; he was not ashamed of my chains, ¹⁷ but when he arrived in Rome he searched for me eagerly and found me— ¹⁸ may the Lord grant him to find mercy from the Lord on that Day—and you well know all the service he rendered at Ephesus.*

Paul prayed God would grant Onesiph'orus mercy for visiting Paul in prison.

### Proverbs19:17 RSV

*He who is **kind to the poor lends to the Lord**, and he will repay him for his deed.*

### Matthew 10:42 RSV

*And whoever gives to one of these little ones even a cup of cold water because he is a disciple, truly, I say to you, he shall not lose his reward."*

## Mark 9:41 RSV

*For truly, I say to you, whoever gives you a cup of water to drink because you bear the name of Christ, will by no means lose his reward.*

## Luke 14:12-14 RSV
## The Parable of the Great Banquet

*He said also to the man who had invited him, "When you give a dinner or a banquet, do not invite your friends or your brothers or your relatives or rich neighbors, lest they also invite you in return and you be repaid.* **13 But when you give a feast, invite the poor, the crippled, the lame, the blind, 14 and you will be blessed, because they cannot repay you. For you will be repaid at the resurrection of the just."**

When is the last time you were told to do this? It does not say when did your church do it or when you gave to some place that did this. It says when **you**. This is when you lay up treasures in Heaven. Most are teaching you how to get increase on earth and how to give for them to fulfill **their** goal, not necessarily God's purpose for you or them. God wants His purpose accomplished through you. Has God told you what your purpose for Him is, or are you being told by a man, religion, or priest?

## Hebrews 6:10-12 RSV

*For God is not so unjust as to overlook your work and the love which you showed for his sake in serving the saints, as you still do. [11] And we desire each one of you to show the same earnestness in realizing the full assurance of* hope until the end, ¹² so that you may not be sluggish, but imitators of those who through faith and patience inherit the promises.

## James 2 :1-9 AMP

*My fellow believers, do not practice your faith in our glorious Lord Jesus Christ with an attitude of partiality [toward people—show no favoritism, no prejudice, no snobbery]. For if a man comes into your meeting place wearing a gold ring and fine clothes, and a poor man in dirty clothes also comes in,*

*³ and you pay special attention to the one who wears the fine clothes, and say to him, "You sit here in this good seat," and you tell the poor man, "You stand over there, or sit down [on the floor] by my footstool," ⁴ have you not discriminated among yourselves, and become judges with wrong motives? 5 Listen, my beloved brothers and sisters: has not God chosen the poor of this world to be rich in faith and [as believers to be] heirs of the kingdom which He promised to those who love Him? 6 But you [in contrast] have dishonored the poor man. Is it not the rich who oppress and exploit you, and personally drag you into the courts of law? 7 Do they not blaspheme the precious name [of Christ] by which you are called?*

*8 If, however, you are [really] fulfilling the royal law according to the Scripture, "You shall love your neighbor as yourself [that is, if you have an unselfish concern for others and do things for their benefit]" you are doing well. 9 But if you show partiality [prejudice, favoritism], you are committing sin and are convicted by the Law as offenders.*

When is the last time you were told to do this? It does not say your church did it or you gave to some place that did this. Denominations divide the body of Christ.

I want to repeat **James 2:24-26 AMP**

*24You see that a man (believer) is justified by works and not by faith alone [that is, by **acts of obedience** a born-again believer reveals his faith].*

*25 In the same way, was Rahab the prostitute not justified by works too, when she received the [Hebrew] spies as guests and protected them, and sent them away [to escape] by a different route? 26 For just as the [human] body without the spirit is dead, so faith without works [**of obedience**] is also dead.*

Rahab believed in God and did a righteous act.

## Rahab Hides the Spies
## Joshua 2:1-14 AMP

*Joshua the son of Nun sent two men as scouts secretly from Shittim, saying, "Go, view the land, especially Jericho [the walled city]." So they went and came to the house of a prostitute named Rahab, and lodged there.* 2 *Now the king of Jericho was told, "Behold, men from the sons of Israel have come here tonight to spy and search out the land."* 3 *So the king of Jericho sent word to Rahab, saying, "Bring out the men who have come to you, who entered your house, because they have come [as spies] to search out all the land."* 4 *But the woman had taken the two men and hidden them; so she said, "Yes, two men came to me, but I did not know where they were from.* 5 *When it was* time to close the [city] gate at dark, the men left; I do not know where they went. Pursue them quickly, for [if you do] you will overtake them." ⁶ But [in fact] she had brought the scouts up to the roof and had hidden them under the stalks of flax which she had laid in order on the roof [to dry]. ⁷ So the [king's] men pursued them on the road to the Jordan as far as the fords [east of Jericho]; as soon as the pursuers had gone out after them, the gate [of the city] was shut.

⁸ Now before the two men lay down [to sleep], Rahab came up to them on the roof, ⁹ and she said to the men, **"I know that the Lord has given you the land,** and that the terror and dread of you has fallen on us, and that all the inhabitants of the land have

melted [in despair] because of you. ¹⁰ *For we have heard how the Lord dried up the water of the Red Sea for you when you came out of Egypt, and what you did to the two kings of the Amorites who were beyond the Jordan [on the east], to Sihon and Og, whom you utterly destroyed.* ¹¹ *When we heard it, our hearts melted [in despair], and a [fighting] spirit no longer remained in any man because of you; for the Lord your God, He is God in heaven above and on earth beneath.*

¹² *And now, please swear [an oath] to me by the Lord, since I have shown you kindness, that you also will show kindness to my father's household (family), and give me a pledge of truth and faithfulness,* ¹³ *and spare my father and my mother and my brothers and my*

*sisters, along with everyone who belongs to them, and let us all live." [14] So the men said to her, "Our lives for yours if you do not tell [anyone about] this business of ours; then when the Lord gives us the land we will show you kindness and faithfulness [and keep our agreement with you]."*

You can see she had faith in the Lord and did works. That's why her faith was alive not dead.

## Salvation Is for All
## Romans 10:5-13 RSV

*Moses writes that the man who practices the righteousness which is based on the law shall live by it. [6] But the righteousness based on faith says, Do not say in your heart, "Who will ascend into heaven?" (that is, to bring*

*Christ down)* ⁷*or "Who will descend into the abyss?" (that is, to bring Christ up from the dead).* ⁸*But what does it say? The word is near you, on your lips and in your heart (that is, the word of faith which we preach);* ⁹*because, if you confess with your lips that Jesus is Lord and believe in your heart that God raised him from the dead, you will be saved.*

¹⁰***For man believes with his heart and so is justified****, and he confesses with his lips and so is saved.* ¹¹*The scripture says, "No one who believes in him will be put to shame."* ¹²*For there is no distinction between Jew and Greek; the same Lord is Lord of all and bestows his riches upon all who call upon him.* ¹³*For, "everyone who calls upon the name of the Lord will be saved."*

## Romans 10:13 AMP

*For "whoever calls on the name of the Lord [in prayer] will be saved."*

**This song totally explains what, "everyone who calls upon the name of the Lord will be saved" means.**

## What a Friend We Have in Jesus
### Joseph M. Scriven, 1855

*What a friend we have in Jesus,*
*All our sins and griefs to bear!*
*What a privilege to carry*
*Everything to God in prayer!*
*Oh, what peace we often forfeit,*
*Oh, what needless pain we bear,*
*All because we do not carry*
*Everything to God in prayer!*

*Have we trials and temptations?*

*Is there trouble anywhere?*

*<u>We should never be discouraged—</u>*

*Take it to the Lord in prayer.*

*Can we find a friend so faithful,*

*Who will all our sorrows share?*

*Jesus knows our every weakness;*

*Take it to the Lord in prayer.*

*<u>Are we weak and heavy-laden,</u>*

*<u>Cumbered with a load of care?</u>*

*Precious Savior, still our refuge—*

*Take it to the Lord in prayer.*

*<u>Do thy friends despise, forsake thee?</u>*

*Take it to the Lord in prayer!*

*In His arms He'll take and shield thee,*

*Thou wilt find a solace there.*

*Blessed Savior, Thou hast promised*

*Thou wilt all our burdens bear;*

*May we ever, Lord, be bringing*

*All to Thee in earnest prayer.*

*Soon in glory bright, unclouded,*

*There will be no need for prayer—*

*Rapture, praise, and endless worship*

*Will be our sweet portion there.*

This was written 167 years ago. If more Christians would do this, their relationship with Jesus would increase dramatically. This is one of the ways to learn to be led by the spirit.

In **Romans 10:10 (KJV)**, *"For with the heart man believeth unto righteousness; and with the mouth confession is made unto salvation."*

For with the heart man believeth unto righteousness and with the mouth confession is made unto salvation are not the same thing.

This word salvation here is a continual work that when you confess with your mouth to Jesus, "I do not know what to do or where to go" and so on, Jesus saves you from the wrong decision by telling you the answer to your question. Even in giving, going, what to wear, and anything else you want direction for from God.

You see, if I ask God should I buy this or not and He says yes, I am not worried about the results positive or negative. I obeyed Him, and the outcome, positive or negative, are His, not mine. It's the same way when you ask Him for directions for anything.  He gets all the glory for positive results and if it does not go the way I was hoping for, it is not my problem because I obeyed **Him.** All the results are His not mine if I obeyed. The results that come when I **do not** ask for directions with my decisions are **mine.**

I am 77 with 8 children at home. My youngest just turned 8. I am working on 48 acres of land that God has me clearing. I just wrote 4 letters to the Joshua generation, working on this one, and one more. Our ministry has a 32,000-square foot furniture store that my family runs where we pray for people all the time. We teach tennis at my house. One of my sons help teach martial arts. Two sons are on the boy's high school tennis team and three daughters are on the girl's tennis team. Seven of them do martial arts five nights a week. Seven nights a week for the last year and a half, we fellowship with God and have each person bring a message from God and a song on their night of the week. My wife is presently home schooling six children, does all the paperwork for our ministry, pays all the bills and much more. Every morning when we get up, we ask God what to focus on today and He directs us. We are at a place in God that if we do not ask for daily direction we would be sinning and would not be saved from not doing what God wants us to do.

## John 3:36 EVS

*Whoever believes in the Son has eternal life; whoever does not obey the Son shall not see life, but the wrath of God remains on him.*

## John 3:36AMP

*He who believes and trusts in the Son and accepts Him [as Savior] has eternal life [that is,* already possesses it]; but he who does not believe the Son and chooses to reject Him, [disobeying Him and denying Him as Savior] will not see [eternal] life, but [instead] the wrath of God hangs over him continually."

## John 1:12 EVS

*But to all who did receive him, who believed in his name, he gave the right to become children of God,*

## John 1:12 AMP

*But to as many as did receive and welcome Him, He gave the right [the authority, the privilege] to become children of God, that is, to those who believe in (adhere to, trust in, and rely on) His name—*

# Apostle Andrew Giannelli

*A messenger of God*

## CONTACT INFORMATION FOR
## APOSTLE ANDREW GIANNELLI
## Email:odm@homesc.com

Apostle Andy and Family

**Charleston, South Carolina**

www.ingramcontent.com/pod-product-compliance
Lightning Source LLC
Chambersburg PA
CBHW071350150726
47997CB00002B/932